AF585208

Australian States *and Territories*

NEW SOUTH WALES

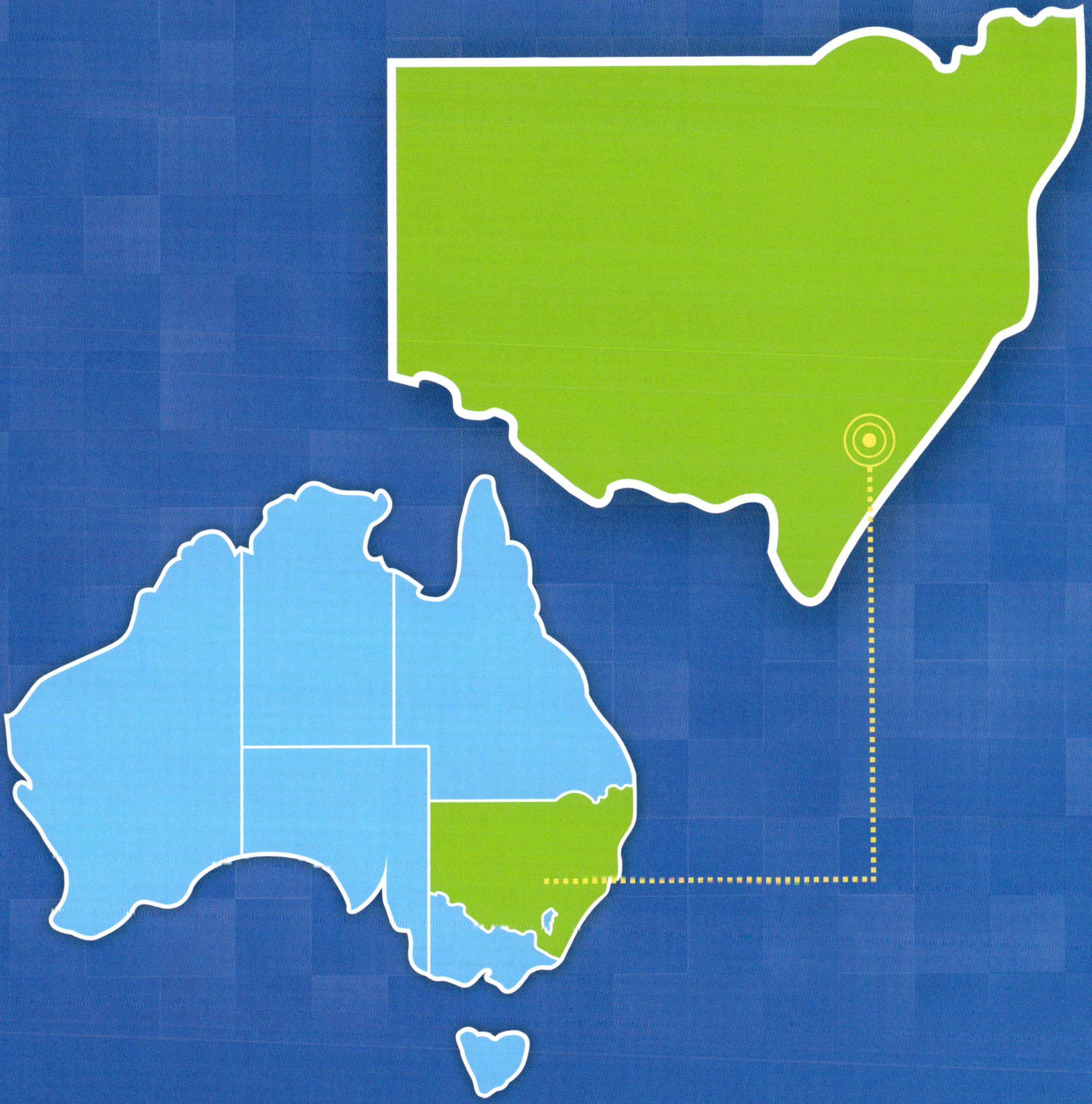

Linsie Tan

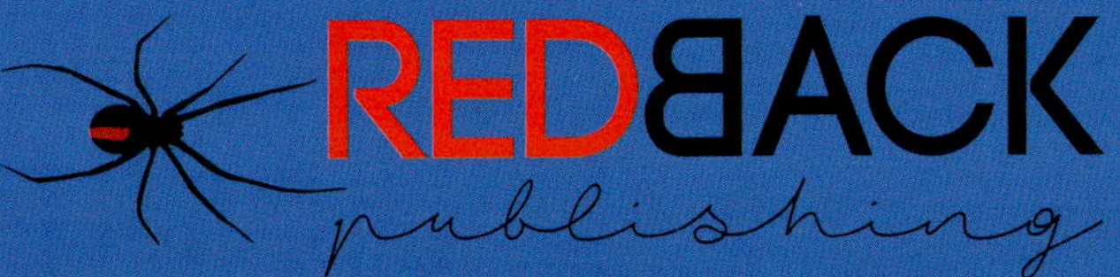

Redback Publishing
PO Box 357 Frenchs Forest NSW 2086
Australia

ISBN 978-0-9946247-1-0

First published 2017
Reprinted 2018

Author: Linsie Tan
Editor: Jane Hinchey
Original illustrations © Redback Publishing 2017
Originated by Redback Publishing
Printed and bound in China by Leo Paper

FSC
www.fsc.org
MIX
Paper from responsible sources
FSC® C020056

Acknowledgements
We would like to thank the following for permission to reproduce photographs: Collections of the State Library of NSW, Mitchell Library and Dixson Galleries, GTS Productions / Shutterstock.com, Robyn Mackenzie / Shutterstock.com, John Elliot Photographer, Squiresy92, Kelly Sturgiss, Punt/Anefo (Nationaal Archief), PH2 Phil Eggman, TimJN1 (Bradshaw Art) and Allan Warren all via Wikimedia Commons and J Bar at English Wikipedia, p28b moman11.

Every effort has been made to contact copyright holders of any material reproduced in this book. Any omissions will be rectified in subsequent printings if notice is given to the publisher.

Cataloguing-in-Publication details are available from the National Library of Australia

CONTENTS

Some words are shown in red, **like this**.
You can find out what they mean by
looking in the glossary.

Geography of NSW

NSW is the fourth largest state in Australia and the capital city is Sydney. The nearest country is New Zealand, which is to the east across the Tasman Sea.

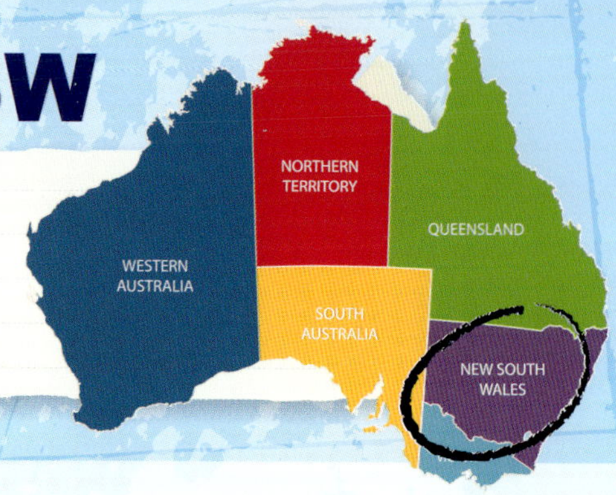

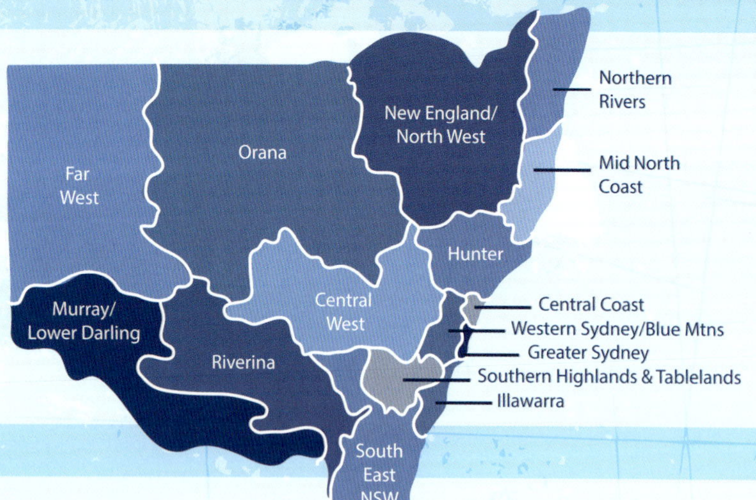

Regional Areas of NSW

Far West, Orana, Murray/Lower Darling, Riverina, Central West, South East NSW, Illawarra, Southern Highlands and Tablelands, Greater Sydney, Western Sydney/Blue Mountains, Central Coast, Hunter, Mid North Coast, Northern Rivers and New England/North West.

Climate

Most of NSW has a temperate climate but there are areas where occasional droughts, floods and extremes of temperature occur.

Indigenous people from the NSW area divided the year into six different seasons, and used them to manage their hunting and travelling.

FAST FACTS

- **Highest recorded temperature: 49.7 °C at Menindie in 1939.**
- **Lowest recorded temperature: -23 °C at Charlotte Pass in 1994.**

Bushfires

Bushfires are a constant threat across the National Parks and other bush areas of NSW. Bushfires can be started by lightning or sometimes by the criminal actions of people who are called arsonists. In 1994, extensive bushfires destroyed large parts of bushland within the Sydney Metropolitan Area and beyond.

Rural Fire Brigades across NSW are staffed by volunteers. The NSW Rural Fire Service is the world's largest vounteer fire-fighting organisation. They fight bushfires, give advice to residents in fire-prone areas, and also undertake controlled burning to reduce the risk of large bushfires.

For thousands of years Aboriginal people used controlled burning to manage the vegetation on their lands.

FIRE DANGER RATING TODAY

LOW-MODERATE · HIGH · VERY HIGH · SEVERE · EXTREME · CATASTROPHIC

· PREPARE. ACT. SURVIVE. ·

Population

NSW has a population of over 7.5 million people. About two thirds of people in NSW live in Sydney. The next highest populations are in Newcastle and Wollongong.

PREDICT THE POPULATION

Draw a graph and use it to estimate what the population will be in 2050.

YEAR	1800	1850	1900	1950	2000	2050
POPULATION of NSW	5,200	267,000	1,360,000	3,241,000	6,485,000	?

FAST FACTS

The longest rivers in NSW are:

- The Darling
- The Murray
- The Murrumbidgee
- The Lachlan
- The Macquarie
- The Namoi
- The Hawkesbury
- The Hunter
- The Macleay
- The Clarence
- The Shoalhaven

Mountains and Tablelands

The highest mountain in Australia is Mount Kosciuszko at 2,200 metres high.

The Great Dividing Range runs along a large part of NSW and separates the coastal lowlands from the western plains. It consists of high tablelands and low mountains and hills. The tablelands provide rich farmlands and pastures.

Coastal Lowlands

The coastal lowlands on the eastern coast feature many beautiful lakes and beaches. The area has fertile soil for farming and is also the most densely populated in the state.

Western Plains

The western plains form two thirds of NSW. They have low rainfall and sparse vegetation. Using careful water control, farmers use this area for crops and for raising livestock.

WORD FILE

temperate - having a mild climate

Origin of Australia Day

Botany Bay in NSW was the first place in Australia where Europeans attempted to form a settlement. After deciding that the land there was too sandy, Governor Phillip moved all the convicts, marines and passengers to another harbour further north, which is where Sydney was founded on 26th January, 1788. This date is now celebrated as Australia Day.

The first arrivals from England

The eleven ships of the First Fleet anchored in the blue waters of the harbour in 1788 and the people were transferred to land.

There were about 1,350 people altogether, and they had been on the ships for eight months. Most of them were convicts who had been sentenced to transportation to the new colony, far away from Great Britain.

The crimes they had committed ranged from violence to stealing small items. Despite this, many convicts lived successful and happy lives in their new land. Their descendants today are proud to have these convicts as their ancestors.

TIME TRAVELLER

Imagine you are one of the convicts on your first night ashore in a new country.

- **Coming from England, what things were immediately different?**
- **After being at sea for more than eight months, how did being on land feel?**

The First Fleet entering Port Jackson, January 26, 1788, drawn 1888 / E. Le Bihan

How they survived

The site where the people of the First Fleet came ashore was near where Circular Quay in Sydney is now. When they arrived, everyone slept in tents or out in the open. They had to work hard to build shelters and search for local food, and it was a long time before they were able to grow the sorts of crops they were used to. They did not know what was safe to eat in the new colony, and the convicts and their guards came very close to starving. Their fresh water came from the Tank Stream, which still runs in pipes under the busy streets of modern Sydney.

FAST FACTS

A convict's food ration

- Salted meat
- Flour
- Peas
- Rice

The Founding of Australia by Capt. Arthur Phillip R.N. Sydney Cove, Jan. 26th 1788

The first farmer

In 1789, James Ruse became the first man to grow wheat in the colony of New South Wales. He was a convict but the Governor was so pleased with his farming skills that Ruse was given land and farm animals for himself. You can still see his property, called Experiment Farm Cottage, at Harris Park near Sydney. The house was built for Surgeon John Harris, who bought the land from Ruse in 1793.

Experiment Farm Cottage

Timeline

the first settlement in Sydney Cove, New South Wales

13th May 1787	11 ships leave England.
18th Jan 1788	First Fleet enters Botany Bay just south of Sydney.
26th Jan 1788	The people are all moved to Sydney Cove and come ashore there.
1789	James Ruse grows the first wheat in the colony.
1792	Starvation is becoming less of a threat and there are 700 hectares of land being cultivated with various crops in NSW.

WORD FILE

transportation - the removal of prisoners from England to NSW in colonial times

Aboriginal History of NSW

Aboriginal people have lived in Australia for at least 60,000 years. They developed complex societies and ways of life, and their culture depends on having strong spiritual connections to the land.

First Contacts

Although the new arrivals from the First Fleet were facing starvation at Sydney Cove in the first years of the colony, the Aboriginal people enjoyed a variety of local bush foods. These included meat from fish and animals, and many plants, fruits and vegetables. They also knew how to use local plants to make medicines. Unfortunately, this skill did not keep them safe from smallpox, which was brought to New South Wales with the new settlers. In 1789, many Aboriginal people died from this illness.

The Aboriginal nations and clans had strong relationships with the land, and this caused conflict between them and the European settlers. Cattle and sheep replaced native food animals on the land, and settlers colonised areas for themselves that had been in traditional ownership for thousands of years.

The Myall Creek Massacre occurred in 1838 in New South Wales when 28 Aboriginal people were killed by a group of settlers. This event resulted in the first convictions of Europeans for crimes against local Aboriginal people.

Opossum Hunting

Notable Aboriginal People in the History of NSW

Portrait of Bennelong

Bennelong
Bennelong was from the Wangal people. He was captured by Governor Phillip, who wanted to learn about the language and customs of the local Aboriginal people. Despite being a captive at first, Bennelong and the Governor soon became friends. The Governor ordered a hut to be built for Bennelong on the area where the Sydney Opera House now stands. Bennelong visited England in 1792. He returned to New South Wales where he died in 1813.

Pemulwuy
Pemulwuy was a warrior of the Bediaga people who lived in the forests beyond Sydney Cove near the Parramatta, Georges and Hawkesbury Rivers. From 1792, he led many attacks against the European settlers, taking food and also spearing people in clashes. He continued this resistance until he was shot dead in 1802. During these years, Pemulwuy developed a reputation for being able to survive any attack, since he had managed to escape from danger so many times.

Aboriginal Nations in NSW

There are many different Aboriginal nations, each with its own lands and cultural traditions. A nation is defined by its connection to its land and by its language. Groups within a nation may also have their own dialects.

FAST FACTS

Aboriginal Nations of the Sydney area	Approximate area covered
EORA	Coastal Sydney area
DHARUG	Parramatta to the Blue Mountains
DHARAWAL	Botany Bay to Nowra
GURINGAI	Sydney North Coast

Aboriginal Nations in NSW

Clarence River Area

Georges River Area NSW 1880

The Wiradjuri is the Aboriginal nation in NSW that covers the largest area of the state. Other large nations in NSW include the Barundji, Wongaibon, Wailwan and Kamilaroi peoples. There are about 47 Aboriginal nations altogether across NSW.

WORD FILE

colonise - to settle in a new land and impose a new culture on the people living there

traditional ownership - the Aboriginal land ownership system in existence before the arrival of Europeans

dialects - different forms of the one language

Colonial History of NSW

New South Wales developed rapidly after 1800. It soon grew into more than just a convict settlement as exploration, farming and the desire for self-government became important to its settlers.

The Exploration of NSW

Free settlers and former convicts were given land by the Governors to encourage them to become farmers. The first Europeans to explore beyond Sydney Cove were looking for more land which settlers could use for crops and raising farm animals to feed the growing colony.

Large areas were later cleared of all trees to provide pastures. The environmental impact of this was to increase the flow of topsoil into rivers, causing many to become clogged with silt. In times of heavy rainfall, flooding of these rivers became a problem. A number of country townships were founded to provide an area of refuge on higher ground for local settlers during times of flooding.

Sydney from Surry Hills, Joseph Lycett, 1819

Gregory Blaxland, William Lawson and W. C. Wentworth

These three men found a way to cross the Blue Mountains in 1813 and discovered that there were vast plains beyond that would be perfect for agriculture. Although there were no roads at this time, Aboriginal people may have assisted these explorers by showing them tracks that were already being used to cross the Blue Mountains.

Charles Sturt

From 1828 to 1830, Sturt explored the inland rivers. Many people thought they must all flow into a large inland sea but he proved this was not the case.

Hamilton Hume and William Hovell

In 1825, Hume and Hovell explored south of Sydney and on towards what was later the state of Victoria. Most of the expedition was paid for by the two men themselves. They discovered extensive areas of grazing land.

George Evans

In 1815, Evans went beyond the Blue Mountains and found the Lachlan and Macquarie Rivers. This was important because it showed that there was enough water to support agriculture. The path he took became the first road to the western farmlands.

The End of Transportation of Convicts

The last ship to bring convicts from England to New South Wales arrived in 1849. After that, other sources of labour were needed to work on farms and in businesses.

Emigrants leaving the ship, Oswald Brierly, 1853

Who Were the Settlers in the Early Colony?

Convicts

Former convicts were encouraged to become farmers and to open businesses. Many were given land and became wealthy after being emancipated.

Solferino Township 1873

Free Settlers

The free settlers felt they were better than the ex convicts, and some were unhappy when Governors gave land and other rights to people who had once been prisoners.

Ministers of Religion

The Church of England was the official religion of the colony, but there were also Roman Catholic priests. Church attendance was compulsory for convicts.

The NSW Corps

These were the soldiers who guarded the convicts. There were no police in the early colony so the NSW Corps took on the role. They became very powerful, and controlled much of the trade in and out of the colony.

Housing

The settlers lived in many different types of housing, depending on how wealthy they were and whether they had convicts or other labourers to help build their houses.

Bark huts - A wooden frame covered in sheets of bark.
Wattle and Daub - A wooden frame plastered with a mixture of straw, manure and soil or clay.
Brick houses - Convicts made bricks from clay.
Stone - Stonemasons built houses and public buildings from local sandstone.

Timeline

Education timeline for New South Wales

- **Before 1788**: Aboriginal children were taught life skills by their families. Boys and girls learned special knowledge at ceremonies marking the end of childhood.
- **1788**: No formal education system existed for European children.
- **1797**: There were a few private schools in the colony.
- **1801**: Female Orphan School opened.
- **1819**: Male Orphan School and first Catholic school opened.
- **1866**: First government schools.
- **1880**: Children had to attend school up to the age of 14.

WORD FILE

emancipation - giving a convict their freedom

Mining and Industry in NSW

The Gold Rush

Edward Hargreaves found gold in 1851 at Ophir near Bathurst. Once this was made public, thousands of people came to the area to look for gold. Roads and townships were built, and many businesses and services flourished as a result of the increase in population. Workers left their jobs to look for gold and their employers were left without enough staff.

TIME TRAVELLER

- You are working in a shop in 1851 and you hear that everyone is becoming rich on the goldfields.

What would you do and why?

Chinese on the Goldfields

The Chinese were the second largest immigrant group searching for gold. In 1860 and 1861, there were riots against them at Lambing Flat, near Young. The government's response was to limit immigration of non-European people into New South Wales.

Left: Small gold minehead without shelter and seven miners, Gulgong

Coal Mining

Coal mining in Australia began in Newcastle in the 1790s, and the first coal was carried in ships to Sydney Cove in 1799. Today, coal is used to produce electricity and is exported to Japan, China and Korea.

Other Minerals Mined

Besides coal, other ores that have been mined in NSW include gold, copper, zinc, silver and lead. Industrial minerals mined have included limestone, brick clay, heavy mineral sands, diatomite, gypsum and magnesium minerals. The gemstone, black opal, is found in NSW as are industrial diamonds.

Many regional centres across NSW owe their origins to mining, including Broken Hill, Wollongong, Cessnock, Muswellbrook, Lithgow, Orange, Gunnedah and Cobar.

Manufacturing

Manufacturing businesses in NSW are involved in a wide range of activities, from making medical devices and producing food to developing and harnessing technology and biotechnology.

NSW has the largest number of defence force faciities in the country. These provide opportunities for manufacturing businesses in areas such as aerospace, electronics, marine, heavy engineering and fabrication.

The Snowy Mountains Scheme 1949-1974

This was the largest engineering project ever undertaken in Australia. The aim was to generate electricity and provide water for irrigation. Many immigrants came from overseas to work on the scheme, building dams, power stations and redirecting whole waterways.

FAST FACTS

Industries in NSW:

- Agriculture & food
- Arts & culture
- Defence & aerospace
- Education
- Financial & professional
- Information & communication
- Infrastructure & construction
- Manufacturing
- Mining & energy
- Tourism

Business and Commerce

The NSW economy is larger than that of a number of nearby countries and it is the largest state economy in Australia. The GDP of NSW makes up one third of the total Australian GDP.

Financial services, such as insurance, banking and stockbroking, are becoming increasingly important to NSW. The Australian Securities Exchange, where shares in listed businesses are traded, is located in Sydney.

WORD FILE

biotechnology - using biology to produce manufactured items

GDP - 'Gross Domestic Product' is a measure of the wealth of an economy

Environment and Sustainability in NSW

Many parts of the natural environment have been destroyed since 1788. Sustainable practices for agriculture and industry require a balance between using the land and waterways for development and keeping areas as regions of natural beauty. The protection of endangered plants and animals is also important.

RESOURCES	HOW WE CAN LOOK AFTER THEM
SOIL	Correct use of fertilisers and avoiding soil erosion and salinity
FORESTS	Using plantations for timber
WATER	Keeping water supplies unpolluted
NATIVE PLANTS	Avoid complete clearing of areas for pastures
NATIVE ANIMALS	Keep some areas of natural bushland for food and shelter
AIR QUALITY	Avoid polluting the air through poor industrial practices

Tourism and the Environment

Tourism is one of the top sources of income for NSW and the industry provides around 350,000 jobs. The NSW National Parks and Wildlife Service manages over 850 national parks or reserves, and works to ensure tourists can enjoy their visit without ruining the areas they have come to see. Businesses offering ecotourism allow tourists to visit an area and be assured they are not going to damage the environment.

Renewable Energy

Renewable energy comes from solar power, wind power and water power.

Water Power - The Snowy Mountains Scheme has been providing power from using flowing water since 1974.

Wind Power - There are a number of windmills across NSW supplying a small proportion of the state's electricity.

Solar Power - Many homes in NSW take advantage of the sunshine by installing solar energy panels.

Protecting Native Plants and Animals

About 100 types of plants and animals in NSW are threatened by extinction. Some of them are:

- The wildlife of the Darling, Lachlan, Murray and Snowy Rivers
- Blue whales, dugongs and southern right whales
- Many frogs and birds
- The long-footed potoroo
- The Wollemi pine

WASTE & POLLUTION

The Environmental Protection Authority in NSW regulates the following sources of waste and pollution:

- Sources of air pollution
- The use of chemicals and pesticides
- Noise pollution
- Radioactive substances
- Other dangerous waste

Dugong

WORD FILE

sustainability - ability of the environment to be used without being destroyed

plantations - farms used to grow one product, such as trees for timber

ecotourism - tourism that does not damage the natural environment

Transport in NSW

Early Methods of Transport

The first methods of transport used by Aboriginal people in Australia were walking and paddling canoes. Canoes were made of bark or from hollowed out logs, and they were used for fishing and to cross rivers and harbours. 'Canoe trees' throughout NSW show large scars where bark was peeled from them. The Australian Museum in Sydney has an example of a bark canoe in its collection.

Aboriginal people travelled to locate food sources, to attend ceremonies and to trade with other groups of people. They had well-known routes which they used for generations.

A stamp printed in Australia shows Cobb & Co. Coach (from etching by Sir Lionel Lindsay).

FAST FACTS

AIRPORTS, ROADS & BRIDGES

- **Kingsford Smith Airport in Sydney is the biggest airport in NSW. There are also many regional airports.**
- **The Newell Highway is the longest road in NSW measuring over 1,000 kilometres.**
- **The Lennox Bridge at Glenbrook is the oldest stone arch bridge in NSW.**

Horses and Coaches

The first settlers walked everywhere or rode horses or in carriages if they could afford them. Cobb & Co coaches pulled by horses became a popular way to go on long journeys in New South Wales before a railway existed. You can see an example of a Cobb & Co coach from 1890 in the Powerhouse Museum in Sydney.

QUICK QUIZ

- **Ferries are an important mode of transport in Sydney. A number of ferries are named after ships in the First Fleet. Can you name them?**

Trains

The first passenger railway line in NSW opened from Sydney to Granville in 1855 using steam trains. Electric trains began running in 1926. Railways made the transport of produce fast and simple, and they contributed to the state's economic development.

River Transport

The rivers in NSW were once important for the transport of people and farm produce. Paddle steam boats were used on the Georges and Parramatta Rivers in Sydney, as well as on the Murray and Darling Rivers. Echuca had a large wharf for loading the paddle steamers that carried most of the wool produced in the area to larger towns where it was sold.

Shipping Ports

Port Botany in Sydney and Port Kembla in Wollongong are the main import and export gateways for commercial ships to NSW. There are also shipping ports at Newcastle, Eden and Coffs Harbour. Most of the commercial fishing in NSW operates from the port at Eden where over 5,000 tonnes of fish are caught each year.

Roads

The early roads in the colony were muddy tracks. As travel and the transport of produce increased, the settlers needed better roads. From 1810, Governor Macquarie used convict workers to build many more roads in the colony.

The first motor cars appeared in Australia in the early 20th century, but the lack of good roads limited the journeys that these cars could undertake. Today, the roads are built and managed by both the NSW state government and by local governments. The Federal government looks after the national highways that link NSW to other states and territories.

Agriculture in NSW

Agriculture is a vital industry in NSW, producing food for local use and for export to other states of Australia and overseas.

Water Supply for Agriculture

All farmers in NSW face periods of flooding and drought, making careful control of the water supply very important. Farmers need licenses to take water from rivers for irrigation, and they also use groundwater from bores. These bores draw from the Great Artesian Basin, a vast underground source of water.

FAST FACTS

NSW farmers are responsible for a large proportion of all the crops grown in Australia:

- **40% of Australia's sorghum crop**
- **32% of Australia's canola crop**
- **29% of Australia's wheat crop**
- **25% of Australia's oat crop**
- **19% of Australia's barley crop**
- **98% of Australia's rice crop**

Crops

Wheat is the major crop grown in NSW in non-drought years. Cotton and rice are also grown across large areas of the state.

Fruit, Vegetables and Wine

A wide variety of fruit and vegetables is grown in NSW. The wine industry, which uses grapes, has recently benefitted from increasing sales in China.

Livestock

Cattle (meat and dairy) and sheep (meat and wool) are the most important livestock in NSW. Other livestock includes poultry, pigs, horses and deer.

The Australian Merino is a breed of sheep that was developed by John and Elizabeth Macarthur near Sydney in the early 1800s. You can visit their historic farmhouse, Elizabeth Farm, at Parramatta. They were responsible for the first wool export to England in 1807.

Elizabeth Farm showing the exact spot where the first sheep were shorn in Australia, 1894

Fisheries

Wild fish, farmed fish and oyster farming contribute $500 million annually to the economy of NSW. A number of fish are thought to be now in such low numbers that catching them for commercial fishing will affect the sustainability of this food resource. These fish and seafood include gemfish, eastern sea garfish, mulloway, eastern king prawn, redfish, school prawn, silver trevally, snapper and yellowtail kingfish.

Forestry

24% of NSW state forests are protected from harvesting. This means that trees cannot be cut down for timber in some areas. From 2005, owners of land in NSW cannot use broadscale land clearing of native forest to produce pastures and fields.

Pine trees and eucalyptus trees are planted on farms to supply the demand for timber in NSW, and to reduce the reliance on imported timber.

Biosecurity

The government in NSW encourages everyone to look after the state's biosecurity to ensure agriculture is not harmed by plant and animal pests, diseases and weeds.

WORD FILE

broadscale land clearing - cutting down all trees in an area
biosecurity - controlling plants, insects and animals that are harmful

Government of NSW

Timeline

UP TO 1788 Australian Aboriginal nations governed according to their own laws.

1770 Captain James Cook explored the coast of eastern Australia and claimed the land for Britain.

1788 Governor Phillip was the highest authority in the colony.

1824 The first Legislative Council met. It assisted the Governor to make decisions about the colony of New South Wales. Its members were chosen by the British government.

1842 Men who owned property could vote for two thirds of the members of the Legislative Council. There were no political parties.

1856 The first time the new Legislative Assembly met. There were now two houses of parliament, as there are today.

1858 Men over the age of 21 could vote as long as they had been born in New South Wales or lived there for 3 years.

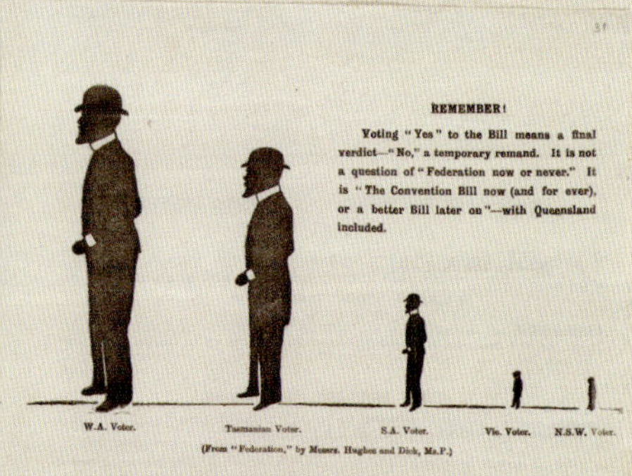

REMEMBER!

Voting "Yes" to the Bill means a final verdict—"No," a temporary remand. It is not a question of "Federation now or never." It is "The Convention Bill now (and for ever), or a better Bill later on"—with Queensland included.

W.A. Voter. Tasmanian Voter. S.A. Voter. Vic. Voter. N.S.W. Voter.

(From "Federation," by Messrs. Hughes and Dick, Ms.P.)

The Constitution Bill rings the death-knell of majority rule.

Forty-one per cent. of the people of the federating States reside in New South Wales. In the course of a few years she will probably contain more than half the population, and contribute at least half the taxation.

But the above Diagram, which indicates (by height of figures) the relative voting strength in the Federal Senate, shows that she occupies the weakest position.

One Tasmanian has eight times the voting power of one New South Wales man.

With nearly half the population and half the taxation N.S.W. will have but one-fifth of the voting strength in the Senate.

WE WANT A FAIR FEDERATION.

Co-operative Printing Works, 237 Castlereagh-st., Sydney.

1901 Federation allowed NSW to become a separate state with its own government.

1902 Women over the age of 30 could vote in NSW.

1925 First woman elected to the NSW parliament.

1928 Women over the age of 21 could vote in NSW.

1962 All Aboriginal Australians could vote in NSW state and federal elections.

1973 People over the age of 18 could vote.

FAST FACTS

'Terra nullius' is Latin meaning 'land that nobody owns'. The British government used this idea to allow them to claim land for the colony of New South Wales.

Colonial Governors and the Rum Rebellion

The soldiers who guarded the convicts were called the NSW Corps. Many of them became wealthy through being allowed to trade using rum instead of money. When Governor Bligh tried to stop them doing this in 1808 they arrested him and took control of the colony themselves.

The NSW Corps stayed in power until the arrival of Governor Macquarie in 1810. This was the only time in Australia's history that there has been an armed rebellion to remove the government.

The arrest of Governor Bligh. Artist unknown, 1808

Sir Henry Parkes, H. B. 1887

Federation

In 1889, New South Wales' Premier Sir Henry Parkes gave a famous speech in Tenterfield. He spoke about all the separate colonies joining together to become a single nation, Australia. He is called the 'Father of Federation'.

The ceremony to create the new Commonwealth of Australia was held at Centennial Park in Sydney on 1st January 1901.

Sir Henry Parkes' Statue, Centennial Park

At the Swearing-in Ceremony, 1901

FAST FACTS

The Federation Pavilion, with all its ornate plaster removed, was later rebuilt in Cabarita Park in the suburbs of Sydney. You can go and see it there and imagine the thousands of people who crowded around it in 1901.

The NSW Parliament Today

There are two sections, or houses, in the NSW parliament. This is called a bicameral system. All members are elected by voters. Laws are made once both houses agree to them.

1. **The Legislative Assembly** - this is also called the Lower House. It has 93 members.
2. **The Legislative Council** - this is also called the Upper House. It has 42 members.

WORD FILE

bicameral - a government having two houses or sections

Notable People from NSW

Government

Edmund Barton (1849 - 1920), the first Prime Minister of Australia, was born in Sydney.

Business

Mary Reiby (1777 - 1855) was convicted in England for stealing a horse. Transported to New South Wales, she later became a very successful businesswoman in the colony, owned many buildings in Sydney, and was a founding member of Australia's first bank.

Sport

Donald Bradman (1908 - 2001) was born in Cootamundra. He is Australia's most famous cricketer.

Dawn Fraser (1937 -) was born in Balmain. She is one of Australia's most famous swimmers, winning gold at three Olympic Games for the 100 metres freestyle.

Yvonne Goolagong-Cawley (1951 -) was born in Barellan. She is the first Aboriginal Australian to compete in tennis at Wimbledon. She won the Women's Singles title in 1971 and 1980, and was ranked number one in the world.

Opera

Joan Sutherland (1926 - 2010) was born in Sydney. Nicknamed 'La Stupenda', she captivated audiences around the world with her exceptional singing skill and performance ability. She was the leading soprano of her time.

MAKE YOUR OWN LIST

Who are three people you think are important in your family, school or suburb?

What makes a person memorable?

Science

Graeme Clark (1935 -) was born in Camden. He invented the bionic ear, which has allowed thousands of deaf people around the world to hear.

Entertainment

Slim Dusty (1927 - 2003) was born is Kempsey and is a legend in country music. His singing and song writing won him many awards. He was responsible for helping to raise the profile of country music and for encouraging young performers to take up singing as their career.

Poetry and Literature

Andrew 'Banjo' Paterson (1864 - 1941) was born in Narrambla near Orange. His famous poem, The Man From Snowy River, has inspired many other artists and writers. Humorous and sentimental, his stories and poems have been admired by all ages.

Jackie French (1953 -) was born in Sydney. She is one of Australia's most awarded writers of children's books. Her books will be found in every children's library across the nation.

Art

William Dobell (1899 - 1970) was born in Newcastle. His unusual portraits upset people who were used to a more realistic style of art. He won the Archibald Prize for portraits three times.

Immigration to NSW

People have come from around the world to live and work in NSW. Their cultures and skills have contributed to the social diversity of the state.

AT LEAST 60,000 YEARS AGO

The ancestors of the Australian Aboriginal people arrived from the north and spread throughout the country.

1788 First Fleet arrived with convicts and their guards.

1793 Five free men and two families arrived to settle.

1840 ONWARDS Migrants from Britain were paid to emigrate to the colonies.

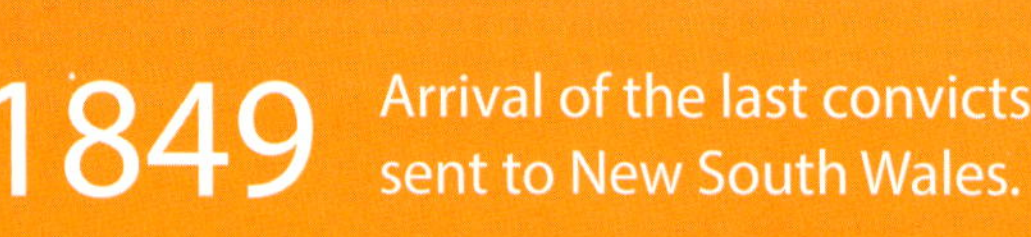

1849 Arrival of the last convicts sent to New South Wales.

1851 The gold rush began to attract thousands of people to New South Wales and helped double its population in only ten years.

1901 The White Australia Policy restricted the arrival of 'non-white' people.

1947 Beginning of the post World War II surge in migrant numbers from Europe.

1975 Vietnamese refugees started arriving after fleeing South Vietnam.

Great Britain

From 1848 to1850 alone, 62,000 free immigrants arrived from Great Britain. Advertisers encouraged young women to make the journey since there was a shortage of women in the colony. Many came from the poorer areas of London, anxious to escape the conditions that had produced the cholera and diphtheria epidemics.

Great Britain remained the source of the largest number of immigrants to NSW until recent years.

Asia

The White Australia Policy restricted all Asian immigration until it was abolished in 1966. Chinese have lived in NSW since the early colonial days, building temples, mining for gold and running businesses. People from India have also been in NSW since the early 1800s.

After the capital of South Vietnam, Saigon, was captured by the North Vietnamese in 1975, Vietnamese refugees came in large numbers to NSW.

New Zealand

New Zealanders making the short journey across the Tasman Sea to Sydney find a way of life that is very similar to the one they have left. Many 'Kiwis' choose to stay as immigrants. Professor Fred Hollows, renowned for his humanitarian work restoring eyesight to thousands, was one of these notable immigrants.

Europe

After the Second World War, refugees and immigrants from Europe came to Australia seeking security and opportunities. The new arrivals were often housed in government hostels in various places throughout NSW. The Snowy Mountains Scheme could not have been completed without the labour provided by migrants from Europe.

DID YOU KNOW?

There are people from over 220 countries in NSW, with the United Kingdom, New Zealand, China and India being the main sources of immigration.

The Middle East

The Lebanese Civil War, 1975 - 1990, led to more than 40,000 refugees coming to Australia.

Refugees from Afghanistan and Iraq are the most recent arrivals to NSW from the Middle East.

Major Sites in NSW

These sites include buildings, structures and natural features. They are important for their beauty, rarity and history.

The Sydney Harbour Bridge

The Harbour Bridge opened in 1932 and is now a symbol of Sydney.

Sydney Opera House

The Opera House is a performing arts centre and an architectural masterpiece.

Hyde Park Barracks, Sydney

The Hyde Park Barracks once housed convicts and is now a museum. The building was designed by convict architect Francis Greenway in 1819.

Bondi Beach and Manly Beach in Sydney

Both of these are popular beaches which symbolise Australia to many visitors from overseas. Governor Phillip named Manly Beach after the proud and fearless Aboriginal men he encountered there in 1788.

FAST FACTS

There are six World Heritage Sites in NSW:

1. Gondwana Rainforests of Australia
2. Greater Blue Mountains
3. Lord Howe Island Group
4. Willandra Lakes Region - includes Lake Mungo archaeological area
5. Four Convict Sites in NSW
   - Old Great North Road
   - Cockatoo Island
   - Old Government House, Parramatta
   - Hyde Park Barracks, Sydney
6. Sydney Opera House

Bondi beach in Sydney

IF YOU WERE THERE NOW

- Look at the photograph of the Sydney Harbour Bridge opening in 1932. Imagine you are walking across the new bridge. What are you thinking as you walk?
- Imagine you are an Aboriginal person living beside Lake Mungo 50,000 years ago, before it dried out and when it was full of fish. As you look across the water, what are you thinking about?

Old Government House, Parramatta

The oldest surviving government building in NSW. Built between 1799 and 1816. Now a museum, the building and its contents reveal the details of daily life in the early colony.

The Blue Mountains

National parks, bushwalking areas and spectacular views make this whole area a well-known tourist destination for locals and visitors to NSW.

Wollemi National Park

The Wollemi Pine, a tree thought to be extinct, was discovered in Wollemi National Park in 1994. The Wollemi Pine has been growing in the area for 100 million years.

Lake Mungo

There is an archaeological site at Lake Mungo that reveals people were living there up to 50,000 years ago. Skeletons found in the sands are the oldest known remains of people to be found anywhere outside Africa.

Flags, Symbols, Emblems and Special Days of NSW

People living in NSW use flags, symbols and special days to show their connection to their community. These connections include pride for the group they belong to, an interest in the history of their group or area, and wanting to join others for celebrations that bring people together.

NSW State Flag

The NSW flag was first used in 1876. It was originally created for use on ships but it has now become a symbol for all of NSW. The Union Jack and the lion remind us of the historic ties to Great Britain. The white badge has four stars that represent the Southern Cross placed on the red cross of St George.

Australian Aboriginal flag

The Aboriginal Flag was first flown in 1971. It was designed by Elder Harold Thomas.
Yellow disc - the sun and yellow ochre
Red - the land
Black - the Aboriginal people of Australia

RULES FOR FLYING THESE FLAGS

- Don't fly more than one on the same pole.
- Don't fly them in the dark.
- Raise the flag to the top of the pole before lowering it to half-mast.
- Treat these flags with respect.

Special Days

Apart from all the national public holidays, there are also some special days that are only held in certain parts of NSW. A few examples are the holidays for the Walcha Cup, the Kangaroo Valley Show and the Albury Gold Cup.

Australia Day - Australia Day is a special holiday for NSW because, as well as being the national day, it commemorates the founding of New South Wales on 26th January 1788.
ANZAC Day - Ceremonies and marches for ANZAC Day are held all around the state on 25th April each year. The largest march in the state is in Sydney and it ends at the ANZAC War Memorial in Hyde Park.
NAIDOC Week - A week in July each year to celebrate the history, culture and achievements of Aboriginal and Torres Strait Islander peoples. Various communities and local and NSW governments organise events around the state for NAIDOC Week.

Symbols of NSW

Floral Emblem - Waratah
Animal Emblem - Platypus
Bird Emblem - Kookaburra
Fish Emblem - Eastern blue groper
Gemstone Emblem - Black opal
Fossil Emblem - Mandageria fairfaxi

The Coat of Arms

This is a symbol of NSW and each part of it has a meaning.

Crest - the rising sun represents the new country
Kangaroo - represents Australia
Lion - represents Britain
Four Stars - represent the Southern Cross
Golden Fleece - represents wealth through sheep farming
Wheat - represents the wheat industry
Motto - 'Orta recens quam pura nites" - these Latin words mean 'Newly arisen one, how brightly you shine'.

Make Your Own Coat of Arms

Design a Coat of Arms for your family, suburb or sport group, etc.

- Use symbols that everyone will know
- Your own Coat of Arms could include drawings or pictures to tell the history of the group
- Think about where to use your Coat of Arms
- What language will you use for a motto?
- Where have you seen the NSW Coat of Arms used?

WORD FILE

Elder - a respected Aboriginal person who is a custodian of traditional knowledge
motto - a few words that express the ideals of a group

How to Find Out More

Primary and Secondary Sources

There are many ways to find out more about NSW. You can do this using both primary and secondary sources. Websites can have a mixture of both types of sources on them.

Primary Sources

- **Interviews** - when people say what they have seen
- **Letters** - when the writer was the person experiencing the event
- **Newspapers** - when the facts are presented
- **Photos** - when they have not been altered
- **Maps**
- **Old Items & Antiques**
- **News on Television** - when it shows pictures of real events or a person saying what they have seen
- **School Newsletters** - when they list names or dates of events
- **Videos on Youtube or Facebook** - when they show an event and have not been altered

Secondary Sources

- **Letters** - when the writer is retelling the facts that someone else told them
- **Newspapers** - when the story is told by someone who retells the facts that someone else told them
- **Photos** - when the photo has been altered
- **Songs, Poems, Stories**
- **News on Television** - when it is reported by a journalist who did not experience the event

Fun Activities Using Sources

- Look up your own suburb in the NSW Hansard and find out what politicians say about it. Go to www.parliament.nsw.gov.au and click on 'Hansard search'.
- Find old newspapers at your local library. Use these to look at pictures of areas you know and see how they have changed over time.

Museums

Visit your local museum to find primary sources. You could look for examples of clothing that the convict labourers wore and compare it with the uniforms of their guards or the dresses owned by the free women settlers.

The Australian Museum

Your Own Family and Friends

Primary sources do not always have to be about famous people. Interviews with your family and friends are important too. Your grandmother might recall what your suburb used to be like. Friends can share stories about coming to live in NSW, either from other states or from a country overseas.

Websites

- The National Library of Australia has made many historic sources searchable online at their website, www.trove.nla.gov.au
- The State Archives of NSW has a website that can be searched for historic information about areas in the state, www.records.nsw.gov.au
- Find out about the search for ancient civilisations at, www.visitmungo.com.au
- Information on Sydney's Aboriginal history is at, www.sydneybarani.com.au
- Visiting old buildings can tell us a lot about the past, www.sydneylivingmuseums.com.au

Glossary

bicameral - a government having two houses or sections
biosecurity - controlling plants, insects and animals that are harmful
biotechnology - using biology to produce manufactured items
broadscale land clearing - cutting down all trees in an area
colonise - to settle in a new land and impose a new culture on the people living there
dialects - different forms of the one language
ecotourism - tourism that does not damage the natural environment
Elder - a respected Aboriginal person who is a custodian of traditional knowledge
emancipation - giving a convict their freedom
GDP - 'Gross Domestic Product' is a measure of the wealth of an economy
motto - a few words that express the ideals of a group
plantations - farms used to grow one product, such as trees for timber
sustainability - ability of the environment to be used without being destroyed
temperate - having a mild climate
traditional ownership - the Aboriginal land ownership system in existence before the arrival of Europeans
transportation - the removal of prisoners from England to NSW in colonial times

Index

www.redbackpublishing.com.au